Holidays

Kwanzaa

by Rebecca Pettiford

Bullfrog Books

Ideas for Parents and Teachers

Bullfrog Books let children practice reading informational text at the earliest reading levels. Repetition, familiar words, and photo labels support early readers.

Before Reading

- Discuss the cover photo. What does it tell them?
- Look at the picture glossary together. Read and discuss the words.

Read the Book

- "Walk" through the book and look at the photos. Let the child ask questions. Point out the photo labels.
- Read the book to the child, or have him or her read independently.

After Reading

- Prompt the child to think more. Ask: Does your family celebrate Kwanzaa? What sorts of things do you see when it's Kwanzaa?

Bullfrog Books are published by Jump!
5357 Penn Avenue South
Minneapolis, MN 55419
www.jumplibrary.com

Library of Congress Cataloging-in-Publication Data
Pettiford, Rebecca.
  Kwanzaa / by Rebecca Pettiford.
    pages cm. —(Holidays)
  Includes bibliographical references and index.
  Summary: "This photo-illustrated book for early readers describes the African-American holiday of Kwanzaa and the things people do to celebrate" Provided by publisher.
  ISBN 978-1-62031-131-8 (hardcover)
  ISBN 978-1-62496-199-1 (ebook)
1. Kwanzaa—Juvenile literature. I. Title.
  GT4403.P48 2014
  394.2612—dc23

                              2013049895

Editor: Wendy Dieker
Series Designer: Ellen Huber
Book Designer: Lindaanne Donohoe
Photo Researcher: Kurtis Kinneman

Photo Credits: Corbis, 12; Derek R. Audette, 13; Exactostock/SuperStock, 22; Hill Street Studios/Blend Images/Corbis, 20–21; Kwame Zikomo/SuperStock, 10–11; Natasha Breen, 6–7; Ocean/Corbis, 16–17; Purestock/Alamy, 4; Rolf Bruderer/Corbis, 5, 8–9; Shutterstock, cover, 1, 3, 23 (all), 24; Shutterstock/ Samuel Borges Photography, 19; Vstock LLC, 14–15; ZUMA Press, Inc./Alamy, 18.

Printed in the United States of America at Corporate Graphics in North Mankato, Minnesota.
3-2014
10 9 8 7 6 5 4 3 2 1

Table of Contents

What Is Kwanzaa?

Kwanzaa begins on December 26.
It is an African-American holiday.

What does
Kwanzaa mean?

It means "first
fruits of the
harvest."

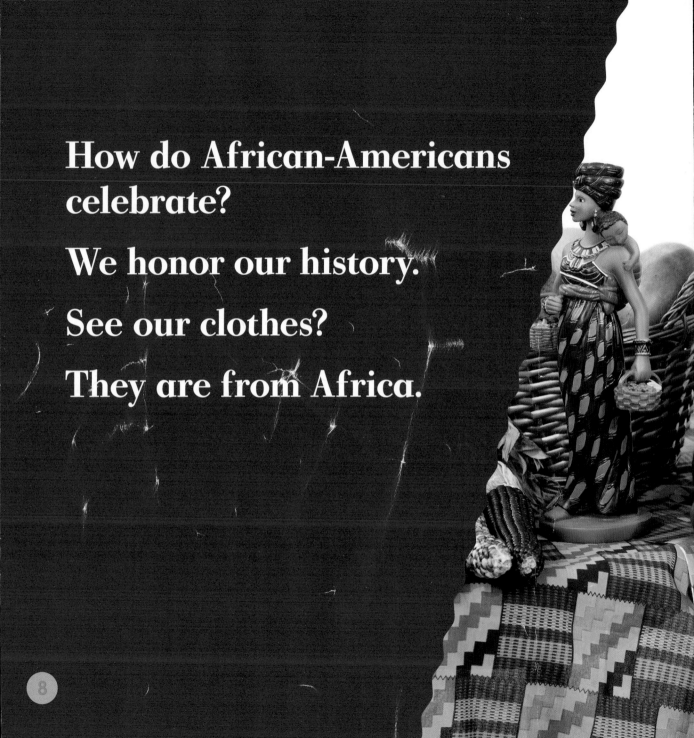

How do African-Americans celebrate?

We honor our history.

See our clothes?

They are from Africa.

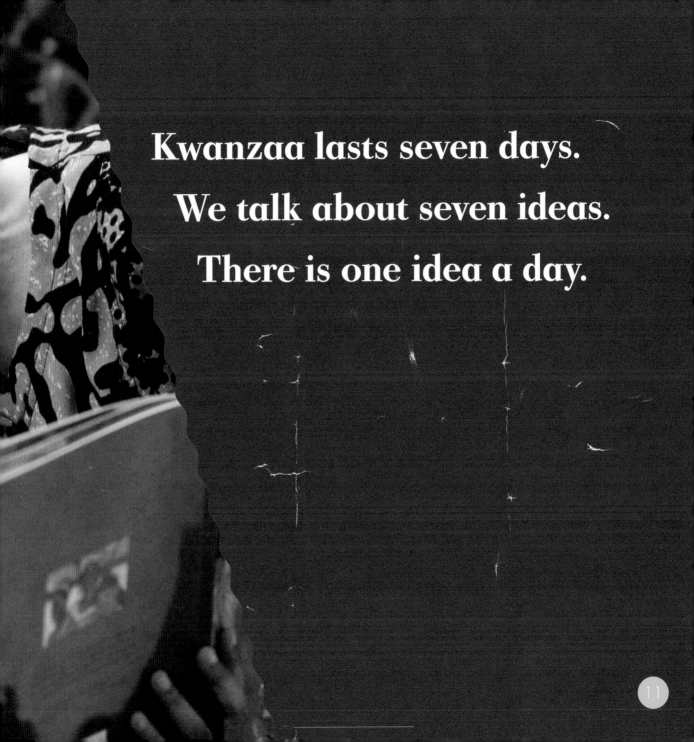

Kwanzaa lasts seven days.
We talk about seven ideas.
There is one idea a day.

Look at our table.

We set out symbols.

Food makes us think of the harvest.

cup

The cup is for family.

We have seven candles.

We light one each day.

They sit in a wood kinara.

kinara ·······▶

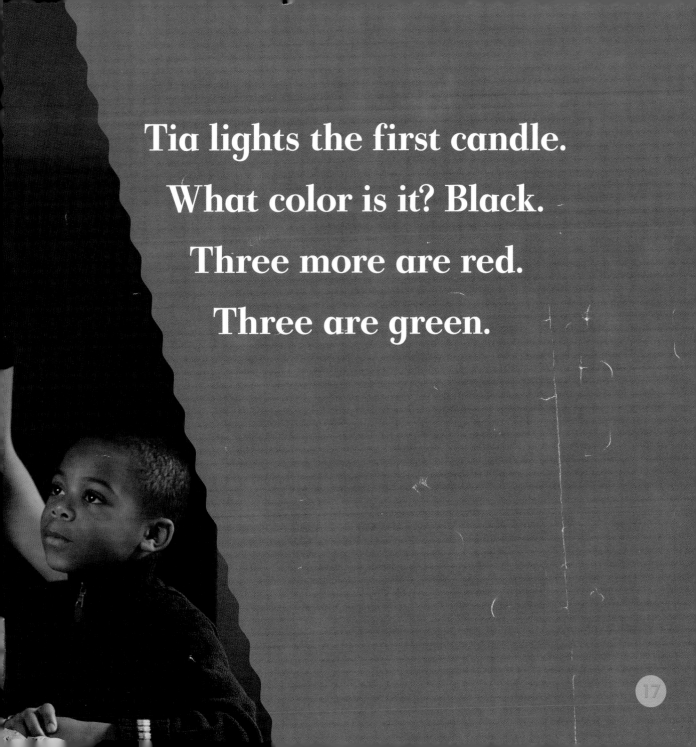

Tia lights the first candle.
What color is it? Black.
Three more are red.
Three are green.

We play music.
Mark plays a drum.

Ana dances.

It's the last day.
Aman gets a gift.
Happy Kwanzaa!

Symbols of Kwanzaa

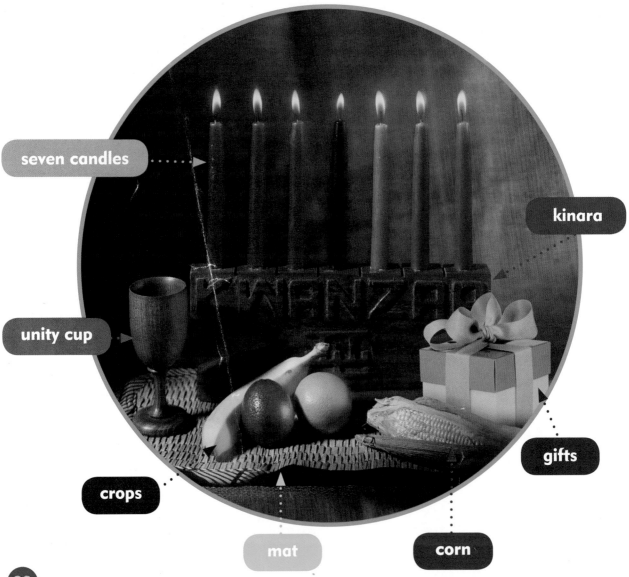

seven candles

kinara

unity cup

gifts

crops

mat

corn

Picture Glossary

Africa
The second-largest continent on Earth; it is south of Europe and Asia.

harvest
The time when large amounts of crops are ripe and are picked or gathered.

African-American
An American whose ancestors were born in Africa.

symbol
An object that reminds us of something else. Crops are a symbol of harvests.

Index

To Learn More

Learning more is as easy as 1, 2, 3.

1) Go to www.factsurfer.com

2) Enter "Kwanzaa" into the search box.

3) Click the "Surf" button to see a list of websites.

With factsurfer.com, finding more information is just a click away.